The **FAA**

Federal Aviation Administration

TRISTAN BOYER BINNS

Heinemann Library
Chicago, Illinois

Published by Heinemann Library,
an imprint of Reed Educational & Professional Publishing,
Chicago, IL

Customer Service 888-454-2279

Visit our website at www.heinemannlibrary.com

Page Layout by Molly Heron
Photo research by Jessica Clark
Printed and bound in the United States by Lake Book
Manufacturing, Inc.

07 06 05 04 03
10 9 8 7 6 5 4 3 2 1

Library of Congress Cataloging-in-Publication Data

Binns, Tristan Boyer, 1968-
  FAA : Federal Aviation Administration / Tristan Boyer Binns.
    p. cm. -- (Government agencies)
Includes index.
  Summary: An introduction to the Federal Aviation
Administration, discussing its nature, structure, and
responsibilities.
  ISBN 1-58810-498-2 (HC),1-58810-982-8 (Pbk)
  1. United States. Federal Aviation Administration--Juvenile
literature. 2. Aeronautics, Commercial--Law and legislation--
United States--Juvenile literature. [1. United States. Federal
Aviation Administration. 2. Aeronautics, Commercial.] I.
Title. II. Series.
  KF2441.Z9 B56 2002
  387.7'0973--dc21

                    2001006746

Acknowledgments
Cover photograph by George Hall/Corbis
p. 1, 11, 16, 21 illustrations of airplane and radar screen by
Guy Palm; p. 2 Doug Armand/Stone/Getty Images; p. 3TL
Jason Reed/Artville; p. 3BR Jack Hollingsworth/PhotoDisc;
p. 4T, 4BL, 12, 13, 21B, 34, 35 Tristan Boyer
Binns/Heinemann Library; p. 4BR Bob Rowan/Corbis; p. 5
Paul Morris/Corbis; p. 6, 7, 8, 9 National Archives and
Records Administration; p. 14, 26, 27, 28, 29T, 38T, 39
FAA/William J. Hughes Technical Center; p. 15, 18B
AP/WideWorld Photos; p. 16, 22, 23 J.P. Carter/Heinemann
Library; p. 17 Roland Herwig/FAA Logistics Center; p. 18T,
19 Civil Aerospace Medical Institute; p. 20T, 20B, 32, 40T,
43 Federal Aviation Administration; p. 20C Patti
Daniel/Northern California TRACON; p. 21T Courtesy of
Raytheon Company; p. 24, 33 Boeing Management
Company; p. 25 Skidmore, Owings & Merrill, LLP; p. 29B
Invision Corp.; p. 30 Eric Gay/AP/WideWorld Photos; p. 31
Bryce Harper/Getty Images/NewsCom; p. 36 NASA; p.
37BL Lockheed Martin Missiles and Space Operations; p. 37
illustrations of Delta rocket and rocket launch by Stephen
Durke; p. 38B Mount Washington Observatory; p. 40B
Young Eagles Experimental Aircraft Association; p. 41 Federal
Aviation Administration/Airbear Program; p. 42T Corbis
Images/PictureQuest; p. 42bB Stockbyte/PictureQuest

Every effort has been made to contact copyright holders of
any material reproduced in this book. Any omissions will be
rectified in subsequent printings if notice is given to the
publisher.

The author and publisher would like to thank the following
for their help: Ned Preston, Tony Debany, Jack Traugott,
Rebecca Trexler, Holly Baker, Roland Herwig, Dick Pollock

Note to the Reader: Some words are shown in
bold, **like this.** You can find out what they mean
by looking in the glossary.

Contents

The FAA's Mission

For thousands of years, humans have wanted to fly. It was not until 1903 that a human finally flew in an airplane. Today, there are more than 230,000 **aircraft.** More than 620,000 people have pilot's **licenses,** and more than 600 million people fly on **commercial** airplanes each year. With so many airplanes flying, the sky could become a huge traffic jam. Instead, a group of workers control how the sky is used. They direct the "traffic"—airplanes— on invisible highways in the sky. These people make sure that all the aircraft and pilots are safe to fly. For more than 75 years, the **Federal Aviation** Administration, or FAA, and other government agencies that came before it have worked to make flying safe and easy.

The FAA is a huge **agency,** with more than 48,000 **employees.** This government agency has many

Most of the FAA's **air traffic controllers** belong to the National Air Traffic Controllers Association.

FAA workers deal with airports and airplanes, both large and small.

important responsibilities. FAA employees work in the United States and with foreign countries to make flying safer and easier. They develop new equipment that can predict, track, and report bad weather so airplanes can avoid it. FAA workers help design airports and **security** systems so both are easy to operate and use. FAA employees also help the environment by working to make airplanes run better and with less noise.

The FAA must work to keep everyone who is involved in flying safe and satisfied—from pilots to air traffic controllers, airlines to **passengers.** It deals with many people in many places, from giant commercial airlines to scientists testing new equipment.

Know It
Watching Weather
Air traffic controllers have to know a lot about the weather so they can plan where airplanes should fly. They use information from weather stations all over the world, looking for storms, lightning, and high winds.

Recent Changes
Only hours after the first **hijacked** jetliner flew into the World Trade Center on September 11, 2001, all of the 4,873 aircraft in the air over the United States had landed. All the airports in the U.S. were closed for days. FAA employees worked very hard to organize better security systems so that the airports could reopen. FAA officials set up new **guidelines** to help prevent **terrorist** attacks in the future. These actions included:

- Sharing information with other government agencies so the backgrounds of workers and passengers can be checked before they get on an airplane
- Checking the security badges of all airport workers
- Helping airlines change **cockpit** doors on airplanes so people can't get through them during flights
- Helping create new security **technology,** such as warning systems between the cabin and the cockpit
- Hiring more federal air marshals to ride on commercial airplanes to help keep passenger and crew safe

How the FAA Began

The United States Postal Service was the first **nonmilitary** government **agency** to use airplanes in an important way. In 1918, the postal service began flying mail across the country. Workers for the postal service created routes in the sky for pilots to follow. They also built lights on the ground to mark the routes so pilots could fly at night and in bad weather.

In 1926, the **federal** government increased its help for private and business pilots. New rules were written for pilots and people who made airplanes to follow. Then the FAA made pilots get **licenses** for themselves and for their **aircraft.** FAA workers also drew maps of the "highways" in the sky to help pilots stay on course.

Pilots discovered that following these highways in the sky was hard. At first, FAA workers built light beacons, or towers. These towers held bright flashing lights so pilots could see them easily from the sky.

This landing field was built in the 1920s. At the end is a tall light beacon with a shed next to it. The shed held the **generator** that made power for the light beacon. A person had to go to each of the light beacons and keep the generators running all the time.

This is thought to be the first airplane registered by the U.S. government. All U.S. aircraft have the letter *N* before their numbers.

Archie League was one of the first **air traffic controllers.** He worked at St. Louis's airport in the late 1920s. He used two flags to tell pilots to land or take off. Here, the flags are rolled up in the wheelbarrow, under his lunchbox.

There were many lights pointing the way along the "highways." Every ten miles (sixteen kilometers) across the country, a pilot could look for a light beacon and know he or she was on course. Every 50 miles (80 kilometers), government workers built a small runway by a light beacon so pilots could land if needed. The lights worked fairly well, but they were hard to see in bad weather. By the late 1920s, the government was putting radio **navigation** aids all over the country. These radio beacons were better than lights because they used radio signals to tell pilots where they were and if they were on course.

During the 1930s, more people were flying. Companies started to use airplanes to carry **passengers** and **cargo.** The government built more runways lined with lights. The government also started using air traffic controllers, who had previously been hired by airports and airlines. Air traffic controllers told pilots where to fly so that airplanes didn't fly into each other.

In the Air and on the Ground

By the 1940s, there were more **air traffic controllers** and more centers where they worked. Controllers used chalkboards or paper strips to list the flights in the air. They tracked the airplanes by using markers on maps and sliding them along as the planes flew. The air traffic controllers did not have radios to talk with the pilots as the planes flew between cities. They had to make telephone calls to airports and airlines and then have the information sent back and forth to the pilots.

Navigation aids were improved during World War II, a conflict that the U.S. entered in 1941. Pilots had more information to help stay on their courses. The **radar** that the **military** started using during the war helped pilots even more. In 1950, the first radar was used to help guide pilots in the United States. Air traffic controllers even started using **radar scopes** to see where airplanes were.

This was the first airway traffic control station, set up in Newark, New Jersey. In 1936, air traffic controllers used map tables, telephones, and chalkboards to track airplanes.

In 1955, the Washington Air Route Traffic Control Center had a radar screen, but air traffic controllers still used little markers on it to show where the airplanes were.

In 1975, air traffic controllers used computers, software, and radar. This system was used at 61 airports in the United States.

New jet engines were invented that allowed aircraft to fly faster. However, even though pilots and air traffic controllers had more and better information, airplanes still collided. The government decided to create a new agency with more power. In 1958, the U.S. government created the **Federal Aviation Agency.** In 1966, the Department of Transportation, or DOT, was created. The Federal Aviation Agency's name was changed to the Federal Aviation Administration, or FAA, and it was made part of the Department of Transportation.

By 1975, FAA workers began using computers with radar information to make a new air traffic control system. Air traffic controllers had much more information to use. More and more flights meant the FAA had to work harder on air traffic control to keep air travel safe.

Over the years, the FAA has taken on more responsibility. Besides its safety work, it now works on noise control, planning airports, and making sure that space vehicles are launched properly.

The Structure of the FAA

The FAA is divided into departments like other U.S. government **agencies.**
There are **human resources, finance,** and computer departments. The FAA
also has some special departments that work on **aviation policy,** talk with
the other government agencies, and deal with the **media.** The person in
charge of the FAA is called the agency's
administrator. But most of the people who
work for the FAA work in one of the six
main "line of business" offices. These are:

- *Air Traffic Services.* Workers here help
  control air traffic.

- *Research and Acquisitions.* Workers here
  are scientists and researchers trying to
  make the airways safer and easier to use.

- *Regulation and Certification.* Workers
  here test pilots and **aircraft** and are
  responsible for giving out **licenses.**

- *Airports.* Workers here help design airports and create safety **guidelines.**

- *Civil Aviation Security.* Workers here protect **passengers** and airplanes.

- *Commercial Space Transportation.* Workers here help plan space launches
  for businesses, such as telephone **satellites.**

There is also an office that oversees the nine **regional** organizations and one
special center. The regional offices each cover a part of the country. The
Mike Monroney **Aeronautical** Center is in Oklahoma. Workers there have
special jobs, such as training **air traffic controllers,** keeping records of pilots
and aircraft, and running testing programs for pilots. There is a second
center in New Jersey, called the William J. Hughes Technical Center.
Scientists there work to make air travel easier and safer.

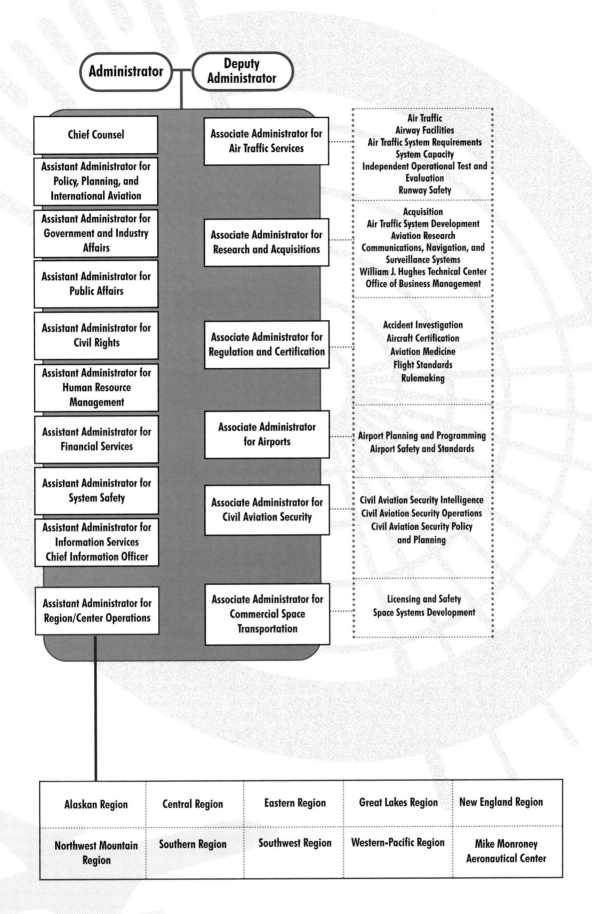

| Administrator | Deputy Administrator |

Chief Counsel

Assistant Administrator for Policy, Planning, and International Aviation

Assistant Administrator for Government and Industry Affairs

Assistant Administrator for Public Affairs

Assistant Administrator for Civil Rights

Assistant Administrator for Human Resource Management

Assistant Administrator for Financial Services

Assistant Administrator for System Safety

Assistant Administrator for Information Services Chief Information Officer

Assistant Administrator for Region/Center Operations

Associate Administrator for Air Traffic Services

Air Traffic
Airway Facilities
Air Traffic System Requirements
System Capacity
Independent Operational Test and Evaluation
Runway Safety

Associate Administrator for Research and Acquisitions

Acquisition
Air Traffic System Development
Aviation Research
Communications, Navigation, and Surveillance Systems
William J. Hughes Technical Center
Office of Business Management

Associate Administrator for Regulation and Certification

Accident Investigation
Aircraft Certification
Aviation Medicine
Flight Standards
Rulemaking

Associate Administrator for Airports

Airport Planning and Programming
Airport Safety and Standards

Associate Administrator for Civil Aviation Security

Civil Aviation Security Intelligence
Civil Aviation Security Operations
Civil Aviation Security Policy and Planning

Associate Administrator for Commercial Space Transportation

Licensing and Safety
Space Systems Development

| Alaskan Region | Central Region | Eastern Region | Great Lakes Region | New England Region |
| Northwest Mountain Region | Southern Region | Southwest Region | Western-Pacific Region | Mike Monroney Aeronautical Center |

FAA Headquarters and Regional Offices

The leaders of the FAA work at the headquarters in Washington, D.C. They are in charge of most large FAA programs. The six "line of business" offices are also based at the headquarters building. Nearly 4,000 people work in the FAA offices in Washington, D.C.

There are nine **regional** offices located in large U.S. cities. Each regional office takes care of the FAA's business in that area. Some regions have more **employees** than other regions. Some regions' headquarters also have offices for groups that help the FAA all over the country. For example, there is an FAA group that checks and **certifies** the safety of engines and propellers for the entire country. This group works in the New England regional headquarters.

The FAA headquarters building in Washington, D.C., is near the White House.

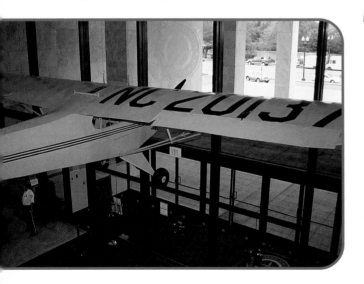

Inside the front doors, visitors can see a Taylor J2 Cub, made in 1936. All visitors must go through metal detectors, like those at airports.

The FAA headquarters even has a day care center for the children of employees. An outside playground is tucked in the back.

This map shows the nine regions of the FAA. Each regional office is responsible for carrying out the FAA's programs in that area.

**ALA
Alaska**

Anchorage

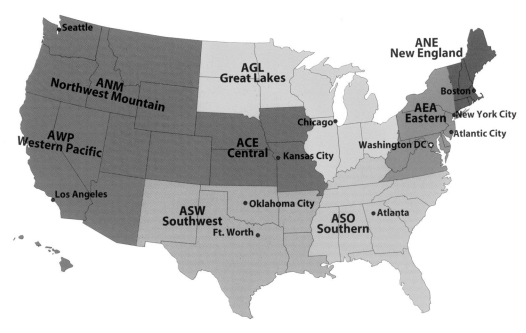

Seattle

**AGL
Great Lakes**

**ANE
New England**

**ANM
Northwest Mountain**

Boston

**AEA
Eastern**

New York City

**AWP
Western Pacific**

Chicago

**ACE
Central**

Kansas City

Washington DC

Atlantic City

Los Angeles

Oklahoma City

**ASW
Southwest**

Ft. Worth

**ASO
Southern**

Atlanta

Technical Wizards

Interesting and exciting things happen every day at the William J. Hughes Technical Center. This is the place where scientists and engineers test **aircraft** and equipment used at airports. The Hughes Technical Center, or "Tech Center," was opened in 1958 as an experimental center. It has kept growing, and today almost 3,000 people work there. Students work there in the summer, learning about the interesting things scientists and **aviators** do.

Workers at the Tech Center use "flying laboratories." These are airplanes that are specially made to test many kinds of in-flight equipment and dangers. Workers study the way weather affects flying and landing. They work on new systems that give more information more quickly and take less time to understand. Workers even find ways to make airplanes run on less fuel.

Tech Center workers also test **air traffic control technology.** They have complicated **simulators** that help teach students how to become air traffic controllers. The simulators look exactly like real air traffic control centers. They even show pictures outside the windows that look like real airports in the United States.

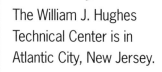
The William J. Hughes Technical Center is in Atlantic City, New Jersey.

These air marshals are taking target practice. They must be very good shots, because firing a gun inside an airplane in flight is very dangerous.

Tech Center workers are trying to make **navigation** easier, too. **Global Positioning System satellites** orbiting Earth can show where an object is anywhere in the world. But workers are trying to improve the system so it can be used by air traffic controllers and in airplane navigation systems. Pilots and air traffic controllers will be able to navigate much more easily and can help keep aircraft safely separated.

Air Marshals

In the 1970s, many airplanes were **hijacked.** To stop these crimes, the FAA required airlines to **screen** all **passengers** so that no one could bring weapons onto an airplane. In 1985, the **Federal** Air Marshal program became a permanent program in the FAA. Air marshals are trained at the Tech Center. They learn how to stop **terrorists.** Air marshals fly secretly on many **commercial** flights. They look just like regular passengers, but they have fake identities, including make-believe families and jobs.

Training and Tracking

The Mike Monroney Aeronautical Center was opened in 1946.

The Mike Monroney **Aeronautical** Center in Oklahoma City, Oklahoma, is a very important place for the FAA. More than 5,000 people work there each day. Many are students who are training at the FAA Academy. About 30,000 students come each year from the United States and foreign countries.

Students at the academy learn:

- to be **air traffic controllers**
- to keep airway equipment, such as **radar** towers, working properly
- to design airports
- to perform safety and **security** checks.

Besides "hands-on" training, students at the FAA Academy also learn in classrooms and on computers.

The center holds information about millions of **aircraft** and **airmen.** Each new aircraft gets an identification number that starts with the letter *N.* Each **certified** airman is **registered,** too. There are records for more than four million airmen. People wishing to work in **aviation** can register there for jobs, such as test pilots and safety **inspectors.**

The center is the FAA's main supply area. All of the FAA's **navigation** and air traffic control equipment must be fixed and maintained. Thousands of extra airplane pieces and parts are stored at the center—enough to cover an area the size of 22 soccer fields. This center also sends people and equipment to natural disaster sites. They try to help keep aircraft flying and landing safely so rescue and relief missions can be flown.

The Civil Aviation Registry at the center gives pilot's **licenses** to all pilots. All aircraft and airmen in the United States cannot fly or work on planes unless they are certified.

Teams of engineers use the many parts stored here at the Mike Monroney Aeronautical Center to fix naviagation and air traffic control equipment.

Medicine in the Air

The Civil Aerospace Institute, known as CAMI, does medical research. The doctors and researchers at CAMI study what happens to people in aircraft accidents. They work to help pilots, **air traffic controllers,** and everyone who works in the dangerous areas of **aviation** to stay safe.

After every airplane accident in the United States, CAMI researchers search the crash sites. They take samples from the people in the airplane. The laboratory at CAMI checks the samples for drugs, alcohol, and dangerous chemicals. CAMI scientists do tests by burning the **materials** used to build airplanes. This will tell them if some materials are safe to use or would be dangerous if breathed in by a pilot or **passenger.** All these studies help to see how people can cause or prevent accidents.

CAMI researchers also test how well aircraft seat belts work. They test emergency systems, such as how quickly people leave the airplane in an accident. CAMI researchers also

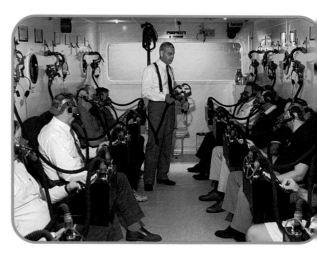

This is a CAMI high altitude chamber. Researchers can create conditions inside the chamber that are exactly like those in airplanes in flight.

Simulators like this one help CAMI scientists learn how pilots work and handle different situations while flying.

In a high altitude chamber, CAMI researchers study what happens to people in different air conditions and when they breath chemicals.

study air traffic controllers. Researchers perform tests to see how being tired affects the way air traffic controllers do their jobs.

Many pilots must have medical exams each year. They must show that they are healthy enough to fly an airplane safely. The doctors at CAMI keep track of the **certificates.** They also train the thousands of doctors who give the exams.

Survival Kit

A good survival kit contains:
- Water
- Food, like granola bars
- Flares to signal to rescuers
- A compass
- A pocketknife
- A first-aid kit
- A rain poncho for shelter
- Waterproof matches

Some pilots are trained to survive in water and freezing temperatures. One survival instructor says, "I am often asked, 'What is the most important piece of equipment to have in a survival situation?' The answer is simple—*You… If you do not have a desire to survive, there is no equipment made that will help you survive.*" By knowing about the areas they fly over, pilots can make special emergency kits to help survive in a crash. They can include items that would be especially useful in the kind of terrain where their planes might go down. For example, a pilot would need extra warm clothing in her survival kit if her plane were to go down in an extremely cold, remote area.

Highways in the Sky

There are about 140,000 takeoffs and landings each day in the United States. That makes for a lot of traffic in the sky. The FAA's Air Traffic Services branch acts like thousands of traffic police and traffic lights. It checks where all the airplanes are and tells them where to go. More than 35,000 people work for Air Traffic Services. More people choose to be **air traffic controllers** than any other job in the FAA.

Directing Flights

1. At the airport, the airplane is controlled by the airport traffic control tower. The pilot is told where to **taxi** on the ground and where and when to take off. The controllers keep all airplanes a safe distance apart.

2. As soon as the **aircraft** is in the air, it contacts a **terminal** area approach control facility, called a TRACON for short. TRACONs handle flights from many airports. They use large radio transmitters like those shown in the picture to stay in communication with pilots.

3. Once the aircraft is beyond the terminal, it is handled by the air route traffic centers. There are 21 of these across the country. One command center looks over all the traffic over the whole country and helps the 21 centers to stop traffic jams in the sky.

4. In flight, several systems help keep the pilot on course and the airplane safe. Flight service specialists record the flight plans the pilot has to file before taking off. They also give the pilot weather reports. Some **radar** tells controllers about bad weather. Other kinds of radar tell them where the airplane is, how high it is, and how fast it is going. The pilot hears signals from radio beacons that tell where the airplane is. Some pilots can also use **satellites** to find out the plane's position.

5. As the airplane prepares to land, it contacts another TRACON, and then the airport traffic control tower. Once the airplane lands safely, radar called "airport surface detection equipment" tells the tower where the airplane is as it moves on the ground.

Know It

Flight plans help people survive after an airplane crash in a remote area. It takes more than 42 hours, on average, for a rescue when there is no flight plan on file with the FAA. But if a flight plan is filed, the average time drops as low as thirteen hours. That is more than a 24-hour difference—an entire day!

A Closer Look: Air Traffic Controllers in Training

Jeff Brennan and Ron Davidson are two **air traffic controllers** in training. Both had **military** training as air traffic controllers before coming to the FAA Academy. Like most students here, they took college courses in air traffic control.

Jeff and Ron say that much of the training is learning how to handle many details. Air traffic controllers must make many important decisions quickly. These decisions affect the safety of **aircraft** and **passengers.**

Every student must take a 25-day class called Air Traffic Basics. Instructors teach students how aircraft fly, how pilots choose their courses, and how to read **navigation** charts. Students also learn about weather basics and how to communicate with pilots in aircraft.

Then students choose the type of air traffic control they want to do. Jeff and Ron both chose "initial **terminal** training." They will learn how to work with flights in the terminal area, including when the airplanes take off and land.

Here, Jeff Brennan listens to his teacher in the classroom.

Looking down on a large model of an airport, a teacher helps Ron direct planes around as he would at a real airport.

These men move model airplanes on the airport model after getting directions from students in the back room.

Computers have become very important in helping air traffic controllers do their jobs. Here, Jeff and Ron train on a computer.

FAA Academy students use **simulators** and train in special laboratories. These help them to better learn what it is like to be an air traffic controller. The basic learning lab uses model airplanes directed by the students. Students must also go to a special classroom where they learn about computers. The FAA Academy even has a room that looks like a real control tower. Practicing there helps prepare students for their future jobs.

If they pass their tests at the end of training, air traffic controllers spend six months to three years continuing to learn while they work.

With so much training, students like to relax in the academy's break room.

Jeff and Ron are proud of their careers as air traffic controllers. Jeff says, "We'll be in training for the rest of our lives, but working with airplanes every day is great!"

Airports

The FAA does not own or operate airports. But FAA workers do have an important role in all airports. The FAA has experts who help build and manage airports. When an airport is planned, the architects and planners follow FAA **guidelines.** These guidelines tell planners the best ways to build the airport.

FAA specialists study how airports are used in the United States. Workers at the FAA and from airports elsewhere study where more airports are needed. They also look at how the noise from airplanes landing and taking off will affect people and animals around the airports.

Got Space?

Airports get too crowded if they run out of runway space. **Commercial aircraft** need long runways to take off and land. The FAA and companies that build aircraft are researching airplanes that take off and land straight up and down, like helicopters do. While flying, the engines on these special aircraft turn so they fly like normal airplanes. If airlines used these types of aircraft, they could schedule many more flights.

JFK: An Airport in Change

John F. Kennedy Airport in New York is one of the busiest airports in the United States. So many flights and people were using the airport that it became too crowded, especially its **Terminal** 4. In 1997, work began to make Terminal 4 bigger and better, so more airlines and **passengers** could use it. When the new terminal is finished it will have:

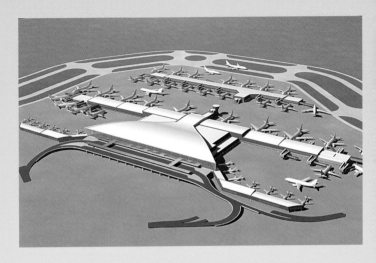

The light rail system will go right into the terminal through holes in the outside wall.

- 16 **gates** and 56 **inspection** areas to handle 3,200 passengers each hour
- 1.5 million square feet (139,500 square meters) of space
- a light rail, or train, system to take passengers to other terminals and to their cars and trains
- gates for new, very large airplanes as well as for smaller airplanes
- specially designed information monitors to help passengers find their gates, bags, and check-in areas more easily

- shorter walks for passengers and less waiting time
- more than 40 stores for passengers
- computerized baggage systems to move bags to the correct places

The new arrivals area will be bright and open, making the terminal seem less crowded.

Airport Science

Scientists working at the FAA study ways to make airports as safe as possible. Some are improving safety checks at airports. Others are researching how new **technology** in **aircraft** affects airports. Researchers must change the way that airports work and how they are designed and built because the aircraft that use airports are changing.

FAA researchers are always trying to improve airport **security**. Today, many airports use systems to find very small amounts of bomb-making materials, called **explosives.** A paper or cotton cloth is used to wipe the object being checked. Then a special machine looks at the cloth to tell if any explosives are there.

Aircraft fires are always a concern at airports. FAA researchers perform special tests on all parts of airplanes to learn more about these fires. Researchers are trying to find better ways to put out fires inside airplanes so **passengers** can get out safely. It is very hard to move through smoke and

FAA researchers study different kinds of airplane fires and test ways to extinguish them.

An enormous pavement-pounding machine slams into a test runway to make sure the pavement won't crack or break when a real plane lands on it.

hot air inside an airplane. Some **materials** used to build airplanes can give off dangerous chemicals if they catch on fire. By inventing new ways to fight these fires, researchers think passengers will be more likely to survive crashes.

Researchers also study runways. Runways are paved, like roads, and they get slippery when wet or icy. Rubber from the tires of thousands of airplane landings and takeoffs wears off onto the runaways. This can also make a runway slippery. FAA scientists study ways to help make runways less slippery.

New aircraft are being built that can carry more and more passengers. This means the aircraft are heavier. Runways must be able to handle these heavy airplanes without breaking or cracking. To help make new runways, the FAA uses computer **simulations** of landing gear, or tires, and runway surfaces. It also has a pavement pounding machine that bangs into the runway like an airplane, so real runways can be tested to see if they hold up.

Keeping People Safe

Safety is the FAA's most important goal. **Security** is a big part of that goal. The Civil **Aviation** Security office works in many ways to improve security. Every person who boards a **commercial** flight in the United States has to go through a security check. Each airport makes its own security plan based on FAA **guidelines.** FAA officials must approve each plan.

All bags that **passengers** carry onto airplanes are x-rayed by a special machine called threat image projection, or TIP. A worker called a **screener** watches the X rays as the bags pass through, looking for dangerous items. There is even a new system that makes sure screeners are doing their jobs.

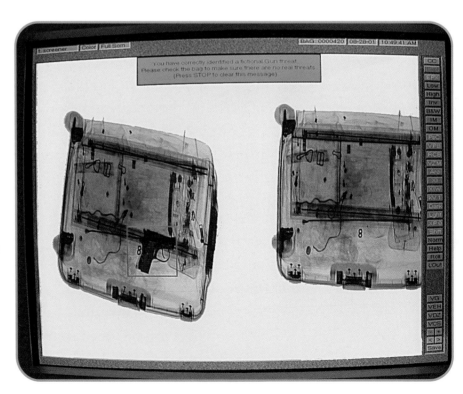

A fake TIP picture tests screeners to make sure that they notice dangerous items such as guns or bombs.

TIP can create a picture of a fake gun or bomb in the real X ray of a bag. The screener has to stop the bag and check it. It's the first good system to check how well screeners are doing.

Even if a bomb is brought into an airport or onto an airplane, the FAA has created ways to keep it from hurting anyone. If a bomb gets on an airplane and can't be removed, the airplane is moved to the "least risk bomb location." Very few people are allowed to go there, and there are no buildings. Today, the FAA is also working on new containers that hold suitcases and other luggage. These containers are made of special **materials** so that an explosion would cause less damage.

Containers like this one may not look special, but they can hold the worst of a bomb blast inside so it doesn't damage the airplane.

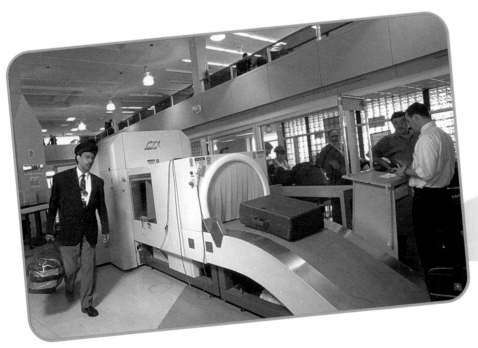

This CAT scan machine looks at all checked bags.

Special Noses

In the 1970s, many airplanes were **hijacked** by **terrorists.** To help stop the hijackings, specially trained dogs were used to stop people from bringing bombs onto airplanes. Dogs can be trained to sniff the chemicals in bombs—known as **explosives.** These dogs sniff for explosives in baggage, in airplanes, in airports, and in cars in parking lots. They can alert their handlers when they find any explosives.

This team is in training. The dog must first learn what the explosives smell like.

Specially trained teams of a dog and a handler work at the large airports in the U.S. Each team trains for about eleven weeks at Lackland Air Force Base in Texas. Trainers at Lackland teach hundreds of teams each year, for the **military** as well as the FAA. When the teams pass the final exams, they begin working. The teams still train each week to improve their skills.

Most handlers are police officers and not FAA **employees.** Their dogs live at home with them. Dogs work for about ten to twelve years. After that, they may continue to live with their handlers.

Later, teams practice hunting for explosives in baggage.

↑ This team is in action at a real airport, looking for explosives inside an airplane.

Other dogs help sniff for illegal foods. They are used in places such as California and Florida. State leaders there want to protect farms and crops from insects or diseases brought in on foods from other places.

There are even some dogs that patrol airports to keep birds away! Birds can cause accidents if they run into **aircraft.**

Four-legged hero

Just minutes after taking off, an airplane was told to land again. It was 1972, and a bomb threat had just been called in. The **passengers** were quickly taken off, and a dog named Brandy was brought on board. Brandy found the bomb only twelve minutes before it was going to blow up. Brandy saved many lives that day. She also showed how well dogs could do an important job.

Safe to Fly

Certification is one of the most important jobs the FAA performs. The Regulation and Certification Division is in charge of all certification. All **aircraft,** airlines, most airports, and everyone who works with aircraft must be certified by the FAA. This means that the FAA makes rules and sets standards that must be followed. Before anyone or anything gets certified, they have to prove that they know the rules, meet the standards, and can do their jobs.

Certification

- All airports where large aircraft take off and land must be certified by the FAA.

- Airlines must show how they will handle emergencies.

- New aircraft need certification before any can be built. Designers and builders work with the FAA to make sure the aircraft will be safe.

- A new aircraft also must be certified when finished to make sure it is safe to fly.

- **Air traffic controllers** are trained at the FAA Academy. But each air traffic control center has different ways of doing its work. So controllers are not certified until they finish training at the place they are going to work.

This FAA **inspector** is checking the inside of a new airplane engine.

Before this style of aircraft could be built, it had to be certified by the FAA.

- Pilots get certified depending on what kind of flying they are trained for. The certificate says what types of aircraft they are allowed to fly and tells if they can fly **passengers** or **cargo** or both.

- Anyone who works on aircraft must be certified. Mechanics are trained at special schools before they get certified.

- The schools where pilots and mechanics are trained, including the teachers, must all be certified.

To keep their certifications, pilots must have medical exams. Aircraft must also be examined by mechanics following FAA **guidelines.** Airlines and airports are inspected to make sure they are following FAA rules.

A Closer Look: Pilot in Training

There are five kinds of pilot **certificates.**

1. Student pilots are pilots in training.

2. Recreational pilots can fly with only one **passenger** and must stay near their home airport.

3. Private pilots can carry more passengers and can use any airport in the country.

4. **Commercial** pilots can be paid to fly passengers or **cargo.**

5. Airline transport pilots can be pilots or copilots for airlines.

Know It

Every pilot must pass a medical exam, a written exam, and a flying exam in order to be certified. It takes between 40 and 55 hours of flight practice before most people are ready to take the exams for the private pilot's certificate.

Flying Lessons

Pilots also get **ratings** that say what type of **aircraft** they can fly. Different airplanes have different ratings.

1. People who want to be pilots must first take flying lessons with a teacher. The first thing in a lesson is a preflight **inspection.** Both the inside and the outside of the airplane need to be checked to make sure it is safe to fly.

2. Once in the airplane, a pilot buckles the safety belt just like in a car. As a student flies more, he or she will get more familiar with the many **instruments.**

3. The airplane has to be driven, or **taxied,** to the runway. It waits in line for its turn to take off. The airplane is steered by pressing pedals in the floor with the feet. Then the student pilot lines the airplane up with the centerline on the runway, gives the airplane full power, and uses the control yoke, or steering device, to lift the airplane off the ground.

4. In the air, students practice moves using the foot pedals and control yoke. They get good at flying straight, flying level, turning, climbing up, and going down.

5. Finally, the student and instructor land the airplane. The instruments tell the pilot how close to the ground he or she is, how fast the plane is moving, and whether the wings are level.

6. After the lesson is over, the airplane gets more fuel. The fuel tanks are in the wings.

Space Launches

The **federal** government launches vehicles and other objects into space, including unmanned rockets and manned space shuttles. These are designed to explore and study space. But some companies also want to launch vehicles into space so they can make money from them. The most common objects launched are **satellites.**

The FAA's **Commercial** Space Transportation office sets safety rules for all private business space launches. Each commercial launch has to be **licensed.** Workers at Commercial Space Transportation decide if the launch will be done safely and will not harm the **national security** of the United States. Then they can give a license to authorize the launch.

The FAA keeps all other aircraft away from launch sites for rockets like this Delta.

Once the company has a license, it can use one of the federal or commercial launch sites. The launch site most often used is the federal Cape Canaveral Air Station in Florida. It's near Kennedy Space Center, where the space shuttles are launched.

Workers at the Commercial Space Transportation office also study space launches. They work on improving launch safety and the safety of the satellites. They research how to build better launch sites and rockets that can be used many times.

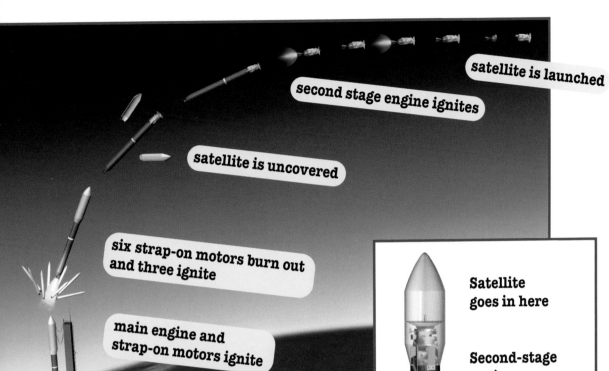

satellite is launched

second stage engine ignites

satellite is uncovered

six strap-on motors burn out and three ignite

main engine and strap-on motors ignite

Satellite goes in here

Second-stage engine

First-stage fuel tank

Strap-on motors

Main Engine

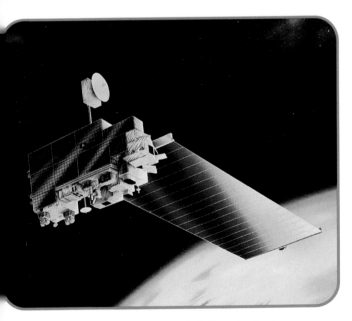

Satellites like this transmit TV and telephone signals and weather information. Satellites are also used for **navigation,** such as for the **Global Positioning System.** Some satellites are used for scientific studies in space.

A rocket, like this Delta ll, is used to launch a satellite into space. The drawing (top) shows the stages in a normal satellite launch.

Moving Forward

Workers in Research and **Acquisitions** study ways to make flying safer. A special drop test facility lets researchers study what happens to airplanes and people during crashes. An entire airplane or just a section of one is lifted and then dropped. During the fall and the impact, **sensors** inside and outside the airplane measure how much stress is felt. Special crash-test dummies are strapped into the seats, like real **passengers** would be. Some of the dummies have sensors, too. These help researchers learn what happens inside an airplane during a crash. They use this information to make new standards so safer airplanes can be built.

Sometimes airplanes can't stop at the end of the runway. Scientists made a special kind of cement that is soft and has air trapped inside it. A large area of this cement called an arrestor bed is built into the end of runways. Airplane tires sink into the arrestor bed, slowing the airplane quickly and safely.

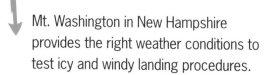

In a test crash, the main body of this airplane section did not break. However, many seats broke, and fuel spilled onto the passenger dummies inside.

Mt. Washington in New Hampshire provides the right weather conditions to test icy and windy landing procedures.

Saving Lives

In May 1999, a small airliner with 30 people on board landed at John F. Kennedy International Airport in New York City. Nearing the end of the runway, the pilot could not stop the airplane. The plane hit the arrestor bed at more than 60 mph (97 kph) and stopped just before it would have fallen into water. Because of the arrestor bed, only one person was injured.

There are many **instruments** that can sense weather conditions. These can send out information to tell **air traffic controllers** all over the country about what's going on. Scientists are always improving their systems that report weather conditions throughout the country. They are also testing systems that measure how far pilots can see in bad weather. Researchers perform ice and snow tests on top of Mt. Washington in New Hampshire. The cold, wet weather on top of the mountain makes it an ideal place to recreate the conditions an airplane would fly through in the winter.

This test airplane took 270 feet (82 meters) to stop, but it landed safely in the arrestor bed.

This FAA scientist is shown next to the tires of the airplane after it stopped. They are almost completely buried in the arrestor bed's special cement.

The FAA Working with People

Some FAA **employees** work with companies and schools to help teach people about flying. These FAA workers hope people will grow to love flying and develop the skills in math and science needed to work in **aviation**. Teachers can get special information on how to teach children about aviation. There is also a group of aviation workers that goes to schools and other places to talk about flying.

The FAA runs the International Aviation Art Contest every year for students ages six to seventeen. Each year has a different theme, and students design posters about the theme. Prizes are given to the students who create the best-looking posters.

FAA officials also work with the Experimental **Aircraft** Association to organize the Young Eagles program. People in the Young Eagles Program are working towards the goal of giving a free flight in a small airplane to one million kids ages eight to seventeen. FAA leaders want to help kids see their

A student from California made this poster for the International Aviation Art Contest. She won first place in the six-to-nine age range for the Western Pacific Region. The theme was "Flight into the Future."

This "young eagle" sits in the **cockpit** of a small airplane before his flight.

Air Bear helps kids learn about all the different workers that help fly an airplane and get **passengers** to their destinations safely.

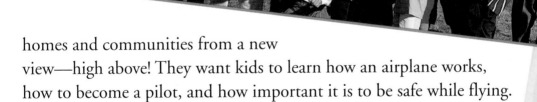

homes and communities from a new view—high above! They want kids to learn how an airplane works, how to become a pilot, and how important it is to be safe while flying.

The Air Bear program is for students in kindergarten through third grade. Air Bear visits classrooms to help kids take a pretend flight. The students all have jobs, from baggage handlers to flight attendants to pilots. They help load and fly the airplane and then land it safely. Students learn about the business of aviation and the careers they could have. They also learn more about how airplanes work, so they may be less scared of flying.

Plans for the Future

The FAA's most important job is to make flying safe. Before the U.S. government became involved in **aviation**, most people were afraid to fly. But FAA rules and **guidelines** now help keep people safe. FAA programs help prepare the teams of people who are responsible for flights. The programs make the workers more aware of how to handle different emergencies.

Maintaining **security**—both in airports and on board **aircraft**—is also an important job for the FAA. FAA researchers are working on new systems to find weapons and **explosives** before they are taken onto any aircraft.

People want to use the air travel system to get where they are going in a timely manner. The FAA is trying to make delays in air travel shorter. Keeping all the equipment is in good condition is one way to help. Also, if all the different people who work together to make a flight happen communicate well to each other, delays will be fewer. Using new **technology** will also help keep flights on time.

Onboard computers and **instruments** help pilots and **air traffic controllers** pick the best routes to fly.

Better-designed airports will help **passengers** travel more safely and quickly.

The number of airline passengers is expected to double to two billion in the next twenty years. That's a lot of extra traffic using the same air space. There is no way to build more highways in the sky, so the FAA is working to move more traffic through the same routes we have now.

New, larger airplanes and better air traffic control systems will help use runway space better. Aircraft will be able to fly closer together in the sky and do it more safely.

Know It

There are more than 50 million aircraft takeoffs and landings in the United States each year.

This wind tunnel at the William J. Hughes Technical Center in New Jersey tests how airplanes react to different wind speeds.

Contacting the FAA

Washington Headquarters
800 Independence Avenue, SW, Room 908
Washington, D.C. 20591
(202) 267-3883

Eastern Region Headquarters (AEA-5)
1 Aviation Plaza
Room 542
Jamaica, NY 11434–4809
Public Affairs Contacts: (718) 553-3015
The Eastern Region covers DE, MD, NJ, NY, PA, VA, WV
Also covers the New England Region (CT, MA, ME, NH, RI, VT)

Great Lakes Region Headquarters (AGL-5)
O'Hare Lake Office Center
2300 East Devon Avenue Room 332
Des Plaines, IL 60018–4686
Public Affairs Contacts: (847) 294-7427
covers IL, IN, MI, MN, ND, OH, SD, WI
and the Central Region (IA, KS, MO, NE)

Northwest Mountain Region Headquarters (ANM-5)
1601 Lind Avenue, SW
Renton, WA 98055–4056
Public Affairs Contact: (425) 227-2015
The Northwest Mountain Region covers CO, ID, MT, OR, UT, WA, WY
Also covers the Alaskan Region

Western-Pacific Region Headquarters (AWP-5)
15000 Aviation Boulevard
Hawthorne, CA 90261
Public Affairs Contact: (310) 725-3580
The Western-Pacific Region covers AZ, CA, HI, NV, Marshall Islands, Mariana Islands,
Singapore, Japan (Yokota), American Samoa, Guam

Southern Region Headquarters (ASO-5)
1707 Columbia Avenue
College Park, GA 30337
Public Affairs Contacts: (404) 305-5100
The Southern Region covers AL, FL, GA, KY, MS, NC, PR, SC, TN, VI

William J. Hughes Technical Center (ACT-5)
Atlantic City International Airport
Atlantic City, NJ 08405
Public Affairs Contact: (609) 485-6253

Mike Monroney Aeronautical Center (AMC-5)
6500 South MacArthur
Oklahoma City, OK 73125–4902
Public Affairs Contacts: (405) 954-7500
Also covers Southwest Region (AR, LA, NM, OK, TX)

Further Reading

Canavan, Andrea. *The Federal Aviation Administration*. Broomall, Penn.:
    Chelsea House Publishers, 2003.

Gunston, Bill. *The World of Flight*. Milwaukee: Gareth Stevens, Inc.: 2001.

Tetrick, Byron. *Choosing a Career as a Pilot*. New York: Rosen Publishing Group, 2001.

Glossary

acquisition something gotten, usually by buying or making it

aeronautical relating to the science of flying

agency part of a government responsible for a certain task

aircraft vehicle that travels through the air

airman government name for a man or woman who works with aircraft

air traffic controller person who directs airplanes in the air and on the ground

aviation the science of flying aircraft

aviation policy decisions and rules about flying made by the government

aviator person who pilots aircraft

cargo goods carried by an aircraft

CAT scan use of an X-ray machine to see inside bags and containers without opening them, used to prevent dangerous items from being brought on board airplanes

certification having a paper that says a person or a machine is able to do something or safe to use

checked baggage bags or luggage carried in a plane's cargo area, not carried by passengers

cockpit area where pilots sit when flying an aircraft

commercial relating to business or done to make money

employee person working for a company or organization

explosive something that explodes or sets off an explosion

federal describing a union of states that share a government

finance science of using money

gate place in an airport where an airplane can meet the terminal

generator machine that produces electricity

Global Positioning System system that uses satellites to tell where anything is on Earth

guideline rule that suggests how to do something correctly

hijack to take control of a vehicle by force

human resources department that has to do with people who work

inspect to examine closely

instrument electrical or mechanical device used to fly an aircraft

license piece of paper or card that gives legal permission to do something

material something used in making another thing

media newspapers, magazines, Internet, books, radio, and television stations—all the things that gather and share information and news

military having to do with the armed forces

national security ways of keeping the country safe

navigation science of figuring out the position and course of an aircraft or ship

nonmilitary not related to the military

passenger person who rides in an aircraft or other form of transportation

radar radio device that sends sound waves that bounce off of objects and return to the device, telling the position and movement of the objects

radar scope televisionlike screen used to look at radar information

rating position within a grading system

regional having to do with a specific area

register written record or list containing details

satellite device that orbits Earth in space

screen to examine closely

security safety from attacks

sensor device that records and measures changes in conditions

simulator device that creates conditions and situations that seem real; often used by people to practice a task or skill

taxi to drive an airplane on the ground

technology use of science and research to improve life

terminal large structure at an airport where many aircraft can pick up or drop off passengers or cargo

terrorist person who uses violence for political reasons

Index